Samsung Galaxy S24 AI Handbook:

Your Ultimate User Guide with fixes
from AI Quirks to Quick Fixes
Everything you Need For Seamless
Samsung Galaxy S24 Use

ELEANOR QUINN

Introduction:

Unlocking the Power of AI in the Samsung Galaxy S24

In the ever-evolving landscape of smartphones, Samsung has once again taken a leap forward with its latest release, the Galaxy S24 series. What sets this flagship apart from its predecessors is the integration of cutting-edge artificial intelligence (AI) features, transforming the way users interact with their devices. In this exploration, we delve into the dynamic world of AI within the Samsung Galaxy S24, unraveling the possibilities and advancements that redefine the user experience.

Overview of Samsung Galaxy S24 AI Features:

The Galaxy S24 series represents a significant stride in leveraging AI to enhance communication, productivity, and creativity. Samsung introduces its comprehensive mobile AI experience under the moniker "Galaxy AI," promising users a universal intelligence on their phones. This move aligns with the industry-wide trend where tech giants are increasingly incorporating AI to distinguish their devices and captivate users in a highly competitive market.

Among the standout features is the AI Live Translate Call, a functionality that provides real-time audio and text translations during phone calls made through Samsung's native phone app. This transformative capability bridges language gaps, offering users seamless communication with individuals speaking different languages. Samsung's commitment to privacy is evident in the processing of certain Galaxy AI features directly on the device, ensuring a secure and efficient user experience.

AI-Centric Processor:

To power these innovative AI features, Samsung has equipped the Galaxy S24 with a state-of-the-art processor. The Qualcomm Snapdragon 8 Gen 3 processor, a powerhouse optimized for AI tasks, empowers the device to execute AI models both locally and in the cloud. This marks a significant technological stride, enabling the smartphone to handle complex AI actions with efficiency. The collaboration between Samsung and Qualcomm underscores a commitment to pushing the boundaries of what AI can achieve on a mobile device.

Building on Previous AI Endeavors:

While generative AI has been making waves across the tech landscape, Samsung has been steadily integrating AI into its smartphones for years.

Features like Bixby Text Call, introduced in early 2023, showcased the company's commitment to enhancing user interactions through AI. Galaxy AI appears to be a natural progression, offering a supercharged and updated version of Samsung's existing AI-driven functionalities. The potential of Galaxy AI extends beyond a mere rebranding, promising a diverse array of AI-powered phone features.

Looking Ahead: As we step into the era of generative AI, Samsung's Galaxy S24 stands as a testament to the company's dedication to early adoption and innovation. While AI has faced scrutiny for gimmicky implementations in the past, the emphasis on practical applications, such as real-time translation and secure on-device processing, positions Galaxy AI as a transformative force. The year 2024 marks a pivotal moment for AI on smartphones, and Samsung's Galaxy S24 is at the forefront, pushing boundaries and redefining the smartphone landscape. Join us on this journey as we unravel the intricacies of the Samsung Galaxy S24 AI features and explore the limitless possibilities they bring to users worldwide.

Chapter 1:

Unpacking the AI Revolution - Understanding the Role of AI in Samsung Galaxy S24

In the realm of smartphones, the Samsung Galaxy S24 series stands as a beacon of innovation, pushing the boundaries of what is possible through the integration of artificial intelligence (AI). As we embark on this journey of exploration, our primary focus is on unraveling the mysteries of the AI revolution within the Galaxy S24, delving into the intricacies that define the role of AI and the transformative Galaxy AI technology.

Understanding the Role of AI:

Artificial Intelligence, once confined to science fiction, has become an integral part of our daily lives. In the context of smartphones, AI has evolved beyond being a mere feature; it is the driving force behind a paradigm shift in user experience. The Galaxy S24 redefines our interaction with technology by introducing AI as a proactive and responsive element, capable of understanding user behavior and adapting in real-time.

The role of AI in the Galaxy S24 extends across various dimensions, including communication, productivity, and creativity. It acts as an intelligent assistant, deciphering user preferences and streamlining tasks for a more seamless and personalized experience. This chapter seeks to demystify the complex interplay between AI and smartphone technology, shedding light on how the Galaxy S24 leverages AI to enhance every facet of user interaction.

Overview of Galaxy AI Technology:

At the core of the Galaxy S24's AI prowess is the revolutionary Galaxy AI technology. This comprehensive suite of

AI-driven features transcends conventional boundaries, offering users a multifaceted and intelligent companion. Galaxy AI is not a singular function but an amalgamation of capabilities designed to augment the user experience.

One standout feature within the Galaxy AI arsenal is the AI Live Translate Call. This groundbreaking functionality enables real-time translation during phone calls, eradicating language barriers and facilitating communication on a global scale. As we unpack the Galaxy AI technology, it becomes evident that its applications extend far beyond language translation. It is a catalyst for creativity, a guardian of privacy, and a facilitator of unparalleled productivity.

Privacy in the Age of AI: On-Device Processing:

As the technological landscape evolves, so do concerns about privacy. The Galaxy S24 addresses these concerns with a forward-thinking approach to AI processing. Certain Galaxy AI features are meticulously designed to operate directly on the device, ensuring that sensitive information remains secure and private. This on-device processing not only safeguards user data but also accelerates the execution of AI-driven actions, contributing to a more responsive and efficient user experience.

From Bixby to Galaxy AI: A Continuum of Innovation:

The journey of AI within Samsung's smartphone ecosystem is not a recent phenomenon. Bixby, Samsung's intelligent assistant, laid the groundwork for the more expansive Galaxy AI. Features like Bixby Text Call, introduced in early 2023, hinted at the possibilities of AI-driven communication. With the Galaxy S24, Samsung takes a leap forward, seamlessly integrating Galaxy AI as an umbrella term for an array of AI-powered functionalities.

The Snapdragon 8 Gen 3 processor, a technological marvel in itself, forms the backbone of Galaxy AI. Unveiled by Qualcomm in October 2023, this processor is optimized for AI tasks, demonstrating Samsung's commitment to utilizing cutting-edge technology to power AI innovations. It signifies not just a chip but a conduit through which the Galaxy S24 channels the transformative capabilities of AI.

Looking Ahead: The Future of AI on Smartphones:

As we navigate the unfolding chapters of this exploration, it's imperative to gaze into the future of AI on smartphones. The Galaxy S24 serves as a vanguard in this narrative, setting the stage for what lies beyond. The AI revolution is not just about features but about shaping a future where intelligence seamlessly integrates into our lives, making technology more intuitive, responsive, and personal.

In the subsequent sections, we will delve deeper into specific Galaxy AI features, unraveling their nuances and unveiling their impact on user interactions. The Galaxy S24 is not just a smartphone; it is a testament to Samsung's commitment to innovation, a canvas where the brushstrokes of AI paint a picture of endless possibilities. Join us as we decipher the intricate language of AI within the Galaxy S24, exploring its depths and embracing the evolution it brings to the world of smartphones.

Chapter 2:

Getting Started - Unleashing the Potential of Your Samsung Galaxy S24 Congratulations on your new Samsung Galaxy S24, a device that not only pushes the boundaries of technological innovation but also introduces you to the incredible realm of artificial intelligence. In this chapter, we will guide you through the initial setup process and help you navigate the AI-enhanced interface, ensuring you make the most of every feature at your fingertips.

Setting Up Your Samsung Galaxy S24

Before you dive into the myriad features of the Galaxy S24, let's start with the basics – setting up your device. Samsung has streamlined the setup process to make it user-friendly, allowing you to get your phone up and running swiftly.

1. Power On and SIM Card Installation:
   - Power on your Galaxy S24 by holding down the side button.
   - Follow the on-screen instructions to select your language and region.

- Insert your SIM card into the designated slot. If you're transferring data from an old device, Samsung provides options to make this process seamless.

2. Connect to Wi-Fi and Samsung Account:
- Connect to a Wi-Fi network to ensure a smooth setup.
- Sign in with your Samsung Account or create a new one. This account is crucial for accessing Samsung's ecosystem of services and maximizing the benefits of AI features.

3. Restore or Transfer Data:
- If you're upgrading from a previous Samsung device or another Android

phone, Samsung's Smart Switch feature lets you transfer apps, photos, and more. Simply follow the prompts during setup.

4. Biometric Security Setup:

- Enhance the security of your device by setting up biometric authentication, such as fingerprint recognition or facial recognition.

5. Samsung Account Integration:

- Link your Samsung Account to seamlessly access services like Samsung Cloud, Galaxy Store, and more. This step ensures a holistic Samsung experience.

Navigating the AI-Enhanced Interface

Now that your Galaxy S24 is set up, let's explore the AI-enhanced interface that makes this device truly exceptional.

1. Intuitive Navigation with One UI:

- Samsung's One UI is designed for effortless navigation. The user interface adapts to your interactions, making one-handed use comfortable.

- Explore the updated icons, smoother animations, and an overall polished design that enhances the visual appeal.

2. Bixby – Your AI Assistant:

- Bixby, Samsung's AI assistant, takes center stage. Use voice commands to perform tasks, ask questions, or control your device. Bixby's integration with Galaxy AI opens up a world of possibilities.

3. Edge Screen for Quick Access:
   - Take advantage of the Edge screen, a curved display feature offering quick access to apps, contacts, and functions. Customize the Edge screen to align with your preferences.

4. AI-Powered Suggestions:
   - Experience the proactive nature of Galaxy AI as it learns from your usage patterns. From suggesting frequently used apps to optimizing settings based

on your habits, enjoy a personalized and intuitive smartphone experience.

5. Enhanced Keyboard Input:
    - The keyboard becomes smarter with AI. Benefit from improved predictive text, autocorrection, and language understanding, making your typing experience more efficient.

As you familiarize yourself with the setup process and the AI-enhanced interface, you're ready to unlock the full potential of your Samsung Galaxy S24. In the next chapters, we'll delve deeper into specific AI features and provide tips for optimizing your device based on your preferences and lifestyle. Get ready to elevate your smartphone experience with the power of AI.

Chapter 3:

Galaxy AI Features in Action – Elevating Your Smartphone Experience

Welcome to the exciting world of Galaxy AI features on your Samsung Galaxy S24. In this chapter, we will explore three standout features – Live Translate Call, Chat Assist, and Circle to Search – each designed to redefine how you communicate, interact, and explore with your smartphone.

Live Translate Call: Real-Time Language Translation

One of the most impressive Galaxy AI features is Live Translate Call, a game-changer for breaking language barriers during phone conversations. Whether you're traveling internationally or connecting with someone who speaks a different language, this feature adds a new dimension to communication.

1. Initiating Live Translate Call:
    - Simply open your Phone app and select a contact.

- Choose the Live Translate option to enable real-time translation during the call.

2. Seamless Multilingual Conversations:

- Experience the magic as the Galaxy S24 translates your words into the recipient's language and vice versa.
- This feature supports translations in multiple languages, fostering smooth and natural conversations.

3. Travel-Friendly Communication:

- Live Translate Call is a valuable companion for travelers, eliminating the language barrier and ensuring you can communicate effectively wherever you go.

Chat Assist: Transforming Text Messages with AI

Chat Assist is a revolutionary feature that enhances your text messaging experience, providing a range of AI-powered tools to elevate your communication style.

1. Changing Tone and Style:
   - Before sending a text message, use Chat Assist to modify the tone or style of your message. Tailor your communication to suit different contexts or recipients.

2. Real-Time Translation:
   - Effortlessly translate text messages into different languages, ensuring clear

communication with friends and contacts worldwide.

3. Spell-Checking Made Easy:
   - Say goodbye to typos with the built-in spell-checking feature. Chat Assist helps you compose messages with confidence and accuracy.

Circle to Search: A Visual Search Experience

Circle to Search introduces a visual and intuitive way to explore the world around you. Whether you want to learn more about objects in photos or discover information visually, this feature brings a new dimension to your smartphone experience.

1. Launching Visual Searches:

   - Open an image in your gallery and activate Circle to Search by holding the home button.

   - Circle any object in the photo that piques your interest.

2. Google-Powered Information:

   - Witness the power of AI as Circle to Search uses Google's technology to provide information about the circled objects.

   - From identifying landmarks to learning about products, this feature turns your photos into gateways to knowledge.

3. Enhanced Product Discovery:

- Shopping becomes more interactive as Circle to Search allows you to find similar products online by circling items in your photos.

- Discover new possibilities and information with a simple gesture.

As you integrate Live Translate Call, Chat Assist, and Circle to Search into your daily smartphone interactions, you'll appreciate how Galaxy AI transforms ordinary tasks into extraordinary experiences. These features are just the beginning – the Samsung Galaxy S24 is your gateway to a future where AI enriches every facet of your digital life. In the following chapters, we'll explore additional AI functionalities and provide expert tips for maximizing their potential. Get ready to embrace the future of smartphone technology with your Samsung Galaxy S24.

Chapter 4:

Productivity Boosters - Unleashing the Power of Galaxy AI

In this chapter, we delve into the productivity-focused Galaxy AI features that elevate your Samsung Galaxy S24 to a versatile tool for both work and creativity. Discover how the Notes App Enhancements, Generative Edit, and Transcript Assist redefine the boundaries of productivity.

Notes App Enhancements: Your Intelligent Note-Taking Companion

The Notes app on the Galaxy S24 receives a significant upgrade with Galaxy AI, transforming it into a powerhouse for efficient note-taking and organization.

1. Format and Summarize with Ease:

   - Leverage the Galaxy AI's Note Assist feature to format and summarize your notes effortlessly.

   - Save time by letting your device organize information into structured and easy-to-follow formats.

2. Digital Covers for Notes:

   - Add a personal touch to your notes with the ability to generate digital covers.

   - Galaxy AI lets you create visually appealing covers that reflect the essence of your notes.

3. AI-Driven Organization:

   - Watch as the Notes app intelligently categorizes and organizes your content, streamlining your note-taking experience.

- With enhanced search capabilities, finding specific information within your notes has never been more intuitive.

Generative Edit: Manipulating Photos with AI Magic

Galaxy AI introduces Generative Edit, a feature that unleashes your creativity by providing powerful tools for manipulating and enhancing your photos.

1. Object Manipulation:
   - Similar to Google's Magic Eraser, Generative Edit allows you to

manipulate and move objects within your photos.

   - Change the composition, erase unwanted elements, and craft visually stunning images with just a few taps.

2. Reflection Removal:

   - Say goodbye to unwanted reflections in your photos.

   - Galaxy AI's Generative Edit includes a feature that intelligently removes reflections, ensuring your pictures are crisp and clear.

3. Creative Freedom:

   - Whether you're an amateur photographer or a seasoned pro, Generative Edit empowers you with creative freedom.

- Experiment with photo elements and achieve professional-looking results without the need for complex editing software.

Transcript Assist: AI-Powered Transcriptions for Seamless Communication

Transcript Assist is an invaluable tool for those who rely on voice recordings and conversations, providing accurate transcriptions and summaries.

1. Transcriptions on the Go:
- Activate Transcript Assist in Samsung's recording app to receive real-time transcriptions of your voice recordings.

- Quickly review and edit transcriptions for meetings, interviews, or personal notes.

2. Summarize Conversations:
- Galaxy AI goes beyond basic transcriptions, offering a summarization feature for lengthy conversations.
- Get concise summaries that capture the essence of your discussions without the need to sift through extensive recordings.

3. Enhanced Accessibility:
- Transcript Assist enhances accessibility by providing written versions of spoken content.
- This feature is a valuable asset for individuals with hearing impairments or

those who prefer written communication.

As you explore the productivity boosters embedded in Galaxy AI, you'll witness how these features seamlessly integrate into your daily tasks, transforming your smartphone into a dynamic productivity hub. The Samsung Galaxy S24 isn't just a device; it's a smart companion that adapts to your needs, making every interaction more efficient and enjoyable. Stay tuned for the next chapter, where we unveil additional AI functionalities that enhance your overall smartphone experience.

Chapter 5:

Photography Magic - Elevating Your Visual Storytelling with Galaxy AI

In this chapter, we embark on a journey through the enhanced camera features of the Samsung Galaxy S24, powered by the magic of Galaxy AI. Uncover the innovative capabilities that redefine smartphone photography, making every shot a masterpiece.

Exploring the Upgraded Camera Features

The Galaxy S24's camera system receives a significant upgrade, delivering stunning visuals and unmatched versatility.

1. 50-Megapixel Telephoto Camera:

- Experience the power of the new 50-megapixel telephoto camera, a remarkable addition that enhances zoom capabilities.

- With 5x optical zoom, capture details from a distance with unparalleled clarity and precision.

2. Sharper Imaging with Titanium Build:

- The Galaxy S24 Ultra introduces a titanium build, ensuring a durable and lightweight device without compromising on strength.

- Enjoy a device that not only performs exceptionally but also boasts a sleek design that complements your style.

3. Brighter Screens for Vivid Viewing:

- Witness an immersive viewing experience with brighter screens reaching up to 2,600 nits.

- From outdoor adventures to indoor entertainment, the Galaxy S24's display ensures vibrant and clear visuals in any environment.

Generative Edit for Photo Enhancement

Galaxy AI's Generative Edit feature isn't limited to just object manipulation; it extends its magic to elevate your photo editing experience.

1. Fine-Tune Your Creations:

- Dive into a world of creative possibilities with Generative Edit's fine-tuning options.

- Adjust lighting, colors, and effects with precision, giving you control over the final look of your photographs.

2. Reflection Removal for Flawless Shots:

- Capture reflective surfaces without the worry of unwanted glare.

- Generative Edit includes a reflection removal tool, perfect for photographers who seek perfection in every shot.

3. Unlock Your Creative Vision:

- Whether you're a photography enthusiast or a casual shooter, Generative Edit unlocks your creative vision.

- Experiment with artistic effects, transform ordinary scenes into extraordinary compositions, and showcase your unique perspective.

The Intersection of Technology and Artistry

The Galaxy S24's camera capabilities, coupled with the intelligent enhancements brought by Galaxy AI, represent the intersection of technology and artistry. As you navigate the upgraded camera features and embrace the creative freedom offered by Generative Edit, you'll discover a new realm of possibilities for visual storytelling.

Stay tuned for the next chapter, where we unravel the immersive experiences crafted by Galaxy AI in gaming, entertainment, and beyond. The Samsung Galaxy S24 isn't just a smartphone; it's a portal to a world where innovation meets imagination, setting a new standard for what a mobile device can achieve.

Chapter 6:

AI Quirks and Quick Fixes - Navigating the Galaxy S24 AI Experience

In this chapter, we delve into the realm of AI quirks, addressing common issues users might encounter and providing quick, effective fixes to ensure a seamless and enjoyable experience with your Samsung Galaxy S24.

Common AI-Related Issues and Solutions

1. Live Translate Call Hiccups:

   - Problem: Occasional translation inaccuracies or delays during Live Translate Call.

   - Solution: Ensure a stable internet connection and speak clearly. Consider updating language models for improved accuracy.

2. Chat Assist Misinterpretations:

   - Problem: Chat Assist occasionally misinterprets the tone or context of text messages.

   - Solution: Provide clear context in your messages, and manually review and adjust suggested changes before sending.

3. Circle to Search Challenges:

- Problem: Difficulty initiating Circle to Search for visual searches.

- Solution: Ensure the photo is well-lit and the object is distinct. Experiment with different angles for optimal results.

4. Note Assist Formatting Issues:

- Problem: Note Assist struggles with formatting and summarizing specific types of content.

- Solution: Manually adjust formatting as needed and offer feedback to Samsung for future improvements.

5. Generative Edit Quirks:

- Problem: Unexpected outcomes or misinterpretations when using Generative Edit on photos.

- Solution: Familiarize yourself with the tool's controls, start with small edits, and refine your technique over time.

Troubleshooting Tips for a Seamless Experience

1. Software Updates:
- Regularly check for software updates to ensure you have the latest AI enhancements and bug fixes.

2. Clear Cache and Data: - If specific AI features act up, clearing the cache and

data for relevant applications can resolve issues.

3. Review App Permissions:

- Ensure that AI features have the necessary permissions to access required resources for optimal performance.

4. AI Learning Period:

- Understand that AI models may improve over time as they learn from user interactions. Be patient, and give the system time to adapt.

5. Community and Support Forums:

- Engage with the Samsung user community and support forums to share experiences and gather insights from fellow users.

Embracing a Glitch-Free Galaxy AI Journey

While AI quirks may occasionally surface, armed with these quick fixes and troubleshooting tips, you'll navigate the Galaxy AI landscape with confidence. Samsung's commitment to continuous improvement means that your Galaxy S24 experience will evolve over time, with updates and refinements enhancing the AI features and addressing user feedback.

Stay tuned for the next chapter, where we explore the integration of Galaxy AI in daily tasks and productivity, unlocking new levels of efficiency and convenience. Your Samsung Galaxy S24 isn't just a smartphone; it's your AI-powered companion on the journey of seamless connectivity.

Chapter 7:

Advanced Customization - Tailoring Your Galaxy S24 AI Experience

In this chapter, we embark on a journey of advanced customization, exploring how users can tailor their Samsung Galaxy S24 AI experience to suit their preferences. We'll delve into the intricacies of integrating Galaxy AI into daily life, unlocking the full potential of AI-powered convenience.

Tailoring Your Galaxy S24 AI Experience

1. Customizing AI Triggers:
   - Explore the settings to define specific triggers for AI features. Tailor when and how certain AI functionalities activate based on your usage patterns.

2. Personalized Chat Assist:
   - Train Chat Assist to better understand your communication style.

Fine-tune the tone and language preferences for more accurate and personalized suggestions.

3. Creating AI Shortcuts:

- Build customized shortcuts to quickly access your favorite Galaxy AI features. Streamline your workflow and save time on routine tasks.

4. Adaptive Learning Preferences:

- Leverage the adaptive learning capabilities of Galaxy AI. Provide feedback on suggested changes and corrections to refine the AI's understanding over time.

5. AI-Enhanced Reminders:

- Integrate AI into your daily reminders. Allow your Galaxy S24 to analyze your schedule and provide context-aware reminders for upcoming tasks and events.

Integrating Galaxy AI into Daily Life

1. Smart Home Integration:
- Connect your Galaxy S24 with smart home devices. Use AI to control lighting, temperature, and other smart home features seamlessly through your smartphone.

2. AI-Driven Fitness Assistance:
- Utilize Galaxy AI to enhance your fitness routine. Receive personalized workout suggestions, nutrition tips, and

performance insights based on your health goals.

3. AI Photography Assistance:
   - Let AI elevate your photography skills. Explore advanced camera settings powered by AI for optimal photo and video capture in various scenarios.

4. Productivity Boost with AI:
   - Integrate AI features into your productivity tools. Leverage AI-powered note summarization, language translation, and transcription for efficient work and communication.

5. AI-Infused Entertainment Recommendations:

- Allow AI to curate personalized entertainment recommendations. Enjoy tailored music playlists, movie suggestions, and content based on your preferences.

Maximizing the AI Advantage

As you dive into the advanced customization options and seamlessly integrate Galaxy AI into your daily life, you'll discover the true power of AI-enhanced experiences. The Galaxy S24 isn't just a smartphone; it's a personalized, intelligent companion that adapts to your unique needs, making every interaction smarter and more intuitive.

Stay tuned for the final chapter, where we explore the future of Galaxy AI, upcoming updates, and how Samsung continues to push the boundaries of AI innovation for an ever-evolving mobile experience. Your journey with the Galaxy S24 is about to reach new heights as you embrace a world where your smartphone becomes an extension of your lifestyle, intelligently powered by Galaxy AI.

Chapter 8:

Future Trends and Updates - Speculations on Upcoming AI Enhancements

As we wrap up our exploration of the Samsung Galaxy S24 AI Handbook, we turn our gaze towards the future. In this chapter, we delve into speculations on upcoming AI enhancements, providing insights into the exciting possibilities that await Galaxy S24 users. Additionally, we discuss strategies for staying updated with Samsung's AI evolution to ensure you're at the forefront of cutting-edge advancements.

Speculations on Upcoming AI Enhancements

1. Evolution of Galaxy AI Features:

   - Anticipate the evolution of existing Galaxy AI features. Speculate on how Samsung might enhance Chat Assist, Live Translate, and other key functionalities with future updates.

2. Integration with Emerging Technologies:

   - Explore the potential integration of Galaxy AI with emerging technologies. Consider how AI might collaborate with augmented reality, virtual reality, or other innovative platforms for a more immersive user experience.

3. Enhanced Personalization Algorithms:
- Speculate on improvements to personalization algorithms. Predict how Galaxy AI might become even more adept at understanding user preferences, behaviors, and context for hyper-personalized interactions.

4. AI-Infused Security Measures:
- Consider advancements in AI-driven security measures. Explore how Galaxy AI could play a pivotal role in ensuring robust security protocols, from

biometric enhancements to advanced threat detection.

5. Collaborations and Partnerships:
   - Speculate on potential collaborations and partnerships. Imagine how Samsung might join forces with other tech giants, AI specialists, or industry leaders to bring novel AI capabilities to the Galaxy S24.

Staying Updated with Samsung's AI Evolution

1. Firmware and Software Updates:
   - Understand the importance of regularly updating firmware and software. Stay informed about the

release of new updates that bring enhanced AI features, security patches, and overall improvements to your Galaxy S24.

2. Community Forums and Feedback Loops:

- Engage with the Galaxy user community. Participate in forums, share feedback, and stay connected with other users to gain insights into real-world experiences and potential AI enhancements.

3. Samsung Events and Announcements:

- Keep an eye on Samsung's official events and announcements. Discover firsthand the latest advancements in Galaxy AI by following keynotes, product launches, and updates from Samsung.

4. Beta Testing Opportunities:
   - Consider participating in beta testing programs. Get a sneak peek at upcoming AI features by joining beta programs, allowing you to experience and provide feedback on cutting-edge functionalities.

5. Tech Insights and Publications:
   - Stay informed through tech insights and publications. Follow industry experts, read tech blogs, and stay abreast of AI trends to gain a deeper understanding of the broader landscape and potential AI advancements.

Embracing the Future

As we conclude our journey through the Samsung Galaxy S24 AI Handbook, we invite you to embrace the exciting future that awaits. Speculations on upcoming AI enhancements pave the way for a dynamic and ever-evolving mobile experience. By staying proactive in your approach to updates and being part of the vibrant Galaxy user community, you position yourself at the forefront of Samsung's AI evolution.

The Galaxy S24 isn't just a smartphone; it's a testament to Samsung's commitment to pushing the boundaries of innovation. The future of AI on your Galaxy S24 holds limitless possibilities, and by staying informed and engaged, you become an integral part of this extraordinary journey. Thank you for joining us on this exploration, and may your Galaxy S24 continue to amaze with each AI-powered interaction.

Chapter 10:

Conclusion - Embracing the AI-Powered Future with Samsung Galaxy S24

As we reach the culmination of the Samsung Galaxy S24 AI Handbook, it's time to reflect on the transformative journey we've embarked upon and envision the boundless possibilities that lie ahead. The Galaxy S24 isn't just a smartphone; it's a portal to a future where artificial intelligence intertwines seamlessly with our daily lives, shaping our experiences in unprecedented ways.

Embracing the AI-Powered Revolution

1. The Evolution of Interaction:

   - The Galaxy S24 marks a significant leap in how we interact with our devices. With Galaxy AI at the helm, mundane tasks become dynamic, conversations become multilingual, and the entire user experience transcends traditional boundaries.

2. From Features to Companionship:

- Beyond the array of features, Galaxy AI becomes a reliable companion, learning from your habits, anticipating your needs, and adapting to your preferences. It's not just about what your phone can do; it's about how well it understands and complements your lifestyle.

3. A Glimpse into Tomorrow:

- The speculations on upcoming AI enhancements provide a tantalizing glimpse into the future. Imagine a world where your phone is not just a tool but a proactive collaborator, enriching your daily routines and presenting solutions before you even recognize the challenges.

A User-Centric Approach

1. User Guide Redefined:

- This handbook goes beyond the conventional user guide. It's not just about technicalities but about empowering you to navigate the AI landscape with confidence. Each chapter serves as a gateway to unlocking the full potential of your Galaxy S24.

2. Troubleshooting Made Seamless:

- Navigating through potential hiccups becomes a seamless process with the troubleshooting tips provided. AI quirks and quick fixes ensure that any bumps in the road are smoothed out, ensuring a consistently delightful user experience.

The Galaxy S24 AI Handbook: Your Companion in the AI Era

As you hold this handbook, you hold more than just a guide; you hold the key to a future where AI seamlessly integrates into your daily rhythm. The Galaxy S24 is not merely a device but an usher into the AI era, where every interaction is an opportunity to explore, create, and connect.

Your AI-Powered Journey Continues

1. Stay Informed, Stay Ahead:

- The final chapter touched upon staying updated with Samsung's AI evolution. The tech landscape is ever-changing, and by staying informed through official announcements, beta testing, and community engagement, you become an active participant in the evolution of your device.

2. Future-Proof Your Experience:

- Embrace the future with open arms. The Galaxy S24 is not just a snapshot in time but a device designed to evolve. By embracing updates, exploring new features, and actively participating in the Galaxy community, you future-proof your AI-powered experience.

A Thank You and Beyond

As we conclude this handbook, we extend our sincere gratitude for joining us on this immersive journey through the AI-powered realm of the Samsung Galaxy S24. May your interactions with your device be intuitive, your explorations be limitless, and your AI-powered experiences be nothing short of extraordinary.

The Galaxy S24 AI Handbook isn't just a manual; it's an invitation to explore, discover, and redefine the way you engage with technology. Embrace the AI-powered future, for with your Galaxy S24 in hand, the possibilities are infinite, and the journey is boundless.

Thank you for being part of this transformative experience.

www.ingramcontent.com/pod-product-compliance
Lightning Source LLC
LaVergne TN
LVHW051608050326
832903LV00033B/4408